AF316682

Elevate Your Essence: The Catalyst of Confidence and Goal Setting

INTRODUCTION

Confidence and goal setting are intertwined within personal development. They coincide together in a dynamic duet, each influencing the other, building upon one another to create a harmonious tune of growth and achievement.

At its essence, confidence is the belief in oneself and one's abilities. It's that voice within us which affirms, "Yes, I can do this." This self-confidence acts as the wind beneath the wings of ambition. Without confidence, our goals, however lofty, remain mere wishes—unanchored and liable to be swept away by the tides of doubt and fear. On the other hand, with confidence, the same goals transform into concrete targets, achievable milestones that we are determined to reach.

Goal setting as a practice, requires a discerning vision—a clarity of purpose. One needs to look into the future and envision a desired outcome, then map out the steps to get there. The act of setting goals itself can be a booster of confidence. When we lay out our ambitions, analyze them, and craft a path forward, we are essentially telling ourselves that the dreams we hold are valid, achievable, and worth pursuing.

Yet, there's a symbiotic relationship between the two. confidence often begets clearer and more ambitious goal setting. When one believes in their capabilities, they are more likely to set challenging goals, pushing boundaries and aiming for heights that seem unreachable to others. This stretches the individual, encouraging growth and fostering even greater self-belief.

Conversely, the very act of achieving set goals, no matter how small, can amplify confidence. Each success, each ticked box is a testament to our capabilities. Every accomplished goal whispers to our psyche, reinforcing the thought that we are competent, capable, and deserving of our dreams. This positive feedback loop between goal attainment and burgeoning confidence can propel individuals to unparalleled success.

However, it's crucial to understand that the journey isn't always linear. There will be setbacks, missed targets, and days when confidence wanes. It's during these moments that the bond between confidence and goal setting is truly tested. Here, the clarity and purpose of our goals can serve as the beacon, guiding us through the fog of self-doubt. It reminds us of our 'why,' urging us to persevere.

In summary, confidence and goal setting share a dynamic relationship. Confidence provides the foundation upon which goals are built, and in turn, the act of setting and achieving these goals fortifies that confidence. Together, they form the pillars of personal development, guiding individuals towards growth, achievement, and fulfillment.

GOAL SETTING

When we try to juggle multiple goals, our attention gets divided. Limiting goals allows us to channel our energy and focus, ensuring that we give each one the attention it deserves. Having a smaller number of goals forces us to prioritize what's truly important. It makes us evaluate our aspirations and narrow them down to the ones that align most with our values and long-term vision.

Pursuing multiple goals simultaneously can be exhausting, both mentally and physically. Spreading ourselves too thin can lead to burnout, reducing the quality of our efforts and hindering progress on all fronts. With fewer goals, we can set realistic and achievable milestones. This not only helps in tracking progress but also boosts confidence because accomplishments fuel our motivation. Fewer goals mean less mental clutter. It helps in reducing the feeling of being overwhelmed. With a clear, concise list, one can approach tasks with a calm and strategic mindset.

When we limit our goals, we're more likely to commit to them fully. With fewer distractions and conflicting objectives, we can dive deeper into each goal, exploring all avenues and strategies to achieve it. In essence, while it might seem counterintuitive, limiting ourselves to fewer goals can enhance our chances of success. It's about quality over quantity, depth over breadth, and focused determination over scattered ambition.

Determine your foremost four goals, be they personal, professional, wellness, or financial. Let's embark on this journey to achieve your aspirations and bolster your confidence.

LET'S BEGIN

In Elevate Your Essence: The Confidence Catalyst of Goal Setting, you hold the key to a profound transformation. This journal is more than a collection of pages—it's your personalized blueprint to unshakable confidence. With each stroke of your pen, you'll etch your aspirations, dreams, and objectives onto the canvas of success.

By embracing strategic goal setting, you're not merely sketching outlines; you're sculpting a masterpiece of self-assurance. This journal is a tool, an ally, and a mentor, guiding you through the exciting journey of realizing your potential. Through the lens of clear, actionable goals, you'll harness the immense power within to conquer doubts, fears, and uncertainties.

Picture a future where you stride with unwavering certainty, where each goal achieved bolsters your confidence, propelling you toward greater heights. Elevate Your Essence is more than a title—it's a promise of self-discovery and self-belief, an invitation to unveil the extraordinary within you.

So, embrace this empowering journey. Write with conviction. Set your goals, chase your dreams, and elevate your essence. Your confidence awaits, and with it, a life filled with accomplishments beyond your wildest imagination. Dare to dream, and let this journal be the beginning of your unstoppable ascent.

List the values that are most important to you.
Reflect on how these values influence your goals
and life direction?

Describe the person you want to become or the life you want to lead. How will achieving your goals help you fulfill this vision?

What are your big dreams and aspirations for the next 5+ years? List them and describe why they are important to you.

my journal

my journal

Break down your medium-term goals into smaller, achievable steps for the next 3-12 months.

LET'S GOAL

Harness the power of intention with clarity. Review your long-term, mid-term, and short-term goals into four pivotal goals for the upcoming month. Whether spanning categories like financial, professional, personal, or spiritual —or perhaps zeroing in on just one area like four financial milestones—it's about zeroing in on what truly resonates. Dive deep, prioritize, and manifest your most coveted outcomes. Your future awaits your focus.

Goal
SETTING

START DATE: ___/___/_____   END DATE: ___/___/_____

MY GOAL IS ...

MY WHY	TO REMEMBER

ACTION STEPS

- ☐ _______________________
- ☐ _______________________
- ☐ _______________________
- ☐ _______________________
- ☐ _______________________
- ☐ _______________________
- ☐ _______________________

THINGS TO USE

- ☐ _______________________
- ☐ _______________________
- ☐ _______________________
- ☐ _______________________
- ☐ _______________________
- ☐ _______________________

DRAW / SKETCH

GRATEFUL FOR

Goal
SETTING

START DATE: __/__/____   END DATE: __/__/____

MY GOAL IS ...

MY WHY	TO REMEMBER

ACTION STEPS	THINGS TO USE
☐ __________	☐ __________
☐ __________	☐ __________
☐ __________	☐ __________
☐ __________	☐ __________
☐ __________	☐ __________
☐ __________	☐ __________
☐ __________	☐ __________

DRAW / SKETCH

GRATEFUL FOR

Goal SETTING

Goal
SETTING

START DATE: ___/___/___   END DATE: ___/___/___

MY GOAL IS ...

MY WHY	TO REMEMBER

ACTION STEPS	THINGS TO USE
☐ _______________	☐ _______________
☐ _______________	☐ _______________
☐ _______________	☐ _______________
☐ _______________	☐ _______________
☐ _______________	☐ _______________
☐ _______________	☐ _______________
☐ _______________	

DRAW / SKETCH

GRATEFUL FOR

Describe your dream life five years from now.
What does your day look like from morning to night?

Describe why now is now its important to work towards your goal, what is your motivation?

my journal

Create a vision board in words, describing images, quotes, and elements that inspire you towards your goals.

List three values that are most important to
you and explain how they align with your
current goals.

my journal

Describe a time you achieved a significant goal. What strategies did you use, and how did it feel to accomplish it?

my journal

my journal

What's one goal that scares you a bit? Why does it scare you, and what steps can you take to overcome that fear?

Describe a time when you stepped out of your comfort zone. How did it feel, and what did you learn that could apply to your current goals?

my journal

Write about a goal you recently abandoned or failed to achieve. What went wrong, and what can you learn from that experience?

my journal

If you could only achieve one major goal in the
next year, what would it be, and why?
Outline a step-by-step plan to achieve it.

my journal

How do your current career goals align with your personal values and long-term vision?

What are your health and wellness goals? How can you make small daily changes to achieve them?

my journal

Identify a goal that aligns with your passion or hobby. How can you pursue this goal while balancing other life commitments?

my journal

What are your financial goals, and what strategies will you use to achieve them?

How do you define success? Write about how
this definition influences your current goal setting.

my journal

How do you handle setbacks, and what strategies can you employ to stay resilient on your goal-setting journey?

my journal

my journal

Identify a goal that requires collaboration with others. How will you foster teamwork and communication?

my journal

Write a mantra or affirmation that encapsulates your goal-setting philosophy.

How will you celebrate your achievements, both
big and small, as you reach your goals?

my journal

Write about a mentor or coach who could help you each your goals. If you don't have one, how could you find one?

Describe how your goals contribute to your community or the greater good.

my journal

What tools or resources do you need to
accomplish your current goals? How will you
acquire them?

my journal

What role does self-care play in your
goal-setting journey? How can you ensure
you maintain balance?

my journal

How do your long-term goals align with your
current daily actions and decisions?

my journal

Write about a cultural, travel, or experiential
goal. How does this add value to your life, and
how will you work towards it?

If you faced no limits or barriers, what would your top three goals be? How can you work towards them ?

my journal

my journal

my journal

my journal

my journal

my journal

Choose a person you admire and write about the qualities or achievements that inspire you. How can you emulate these in your own life?

my journal

What habits or routines could you establish to move closer to your short-term goals? Outline a plan for incorporating them into your daily life.

What obstacles have hindered your progress towards your goals in the past? How can you overcome these obstacles in the future?

my journal

Who are the key people that can support you in
reaching your goals? How can they assist you,
and how will you reach out to them?

MONTHLY REFLECTION

DATE: TIME:

✦ Monthly Wins

____

____

✦ Challenges

____

____

✦ How does it make me feel?

____

____

✦ How can I improve it?

____

____

Accomplished Goals	Unaccomplished Goals	Goals Next Month

Habits Retained	Habits Eliminated	New Habits Developed (Good & Bad)

Three things that I am most grateful for this month:

Two life lessons I learned this month:

____

One word that best describes this month:

____

How will you rate this month?   ☆☆☆☆☆

List the values that are most important to you.
Reflect on how these values influence your
goals and life direction.

my journal

Describe the person you want to become or the life you want to lead. How will achieving your goals help you fulfill this vision?

my journal

Write down your weekly targets that align with your short-term goals.

my journal

Reflect on your progress, make necessary adjustments to your plan, and celebrate your achievements.

What are your goals for the next 1-5 years? How do they align with your long-term vision?

my journal

my journal

Collect inspiring quotes, images, or notes that keep you motivated. List a few.

MONTHLY REFLECTION

DATE: TIME:

✦ Monthly Wins

____
____

✦ Challenges

____
____

✦ How does it make me feel?

____
____

✦ How can I improve it?

____
____

Accomplished Goals   Unaccomplished Goals   Goals Next Month

______________   ______________   ______________

Habits Retained   Habits Eliminated   New Habits Developed
(Good & Bad)

______________   ______________   ______________

Three things that I am most grateful for this month:

Two life lessons I learned this month:

____

One word that best describes this month:

____

How will you rate this month?   ☆☆☆☆☆

Outline the habits and routines you'll adopt to continually improve yourself. How will you enhance your discipline and resilience? Detail the steps you'll take to cultivate a mindset of continuous growth and self-mastery.

my journal

Describe a day in your ideal life that balances work, leisure, and personal growth. How will you allocate your time and energy to ensure a fulfilling and harmonious lifestyle that aligns with your values and goals?

my journal

Define the knowledge and skills you wish to acquire. What subjects, languages, or expertise do you aspire to possess? Lay out a roadmap for continuous learning and development, fostering intellectual growth and curiosity.

my journal

Identify one fear that has been holding you back.
Write about the actions you'll take to confront
and conquer this fear, allowing courage to guide
you towards a life of bold choices and unbounded
possibilities.

my journal

Envision the quality of relationships you desire in your life. Who are the people you want to surround yourself with? Describe the qualities of these relationships and how you'll invest in them to create a network of meaningful connections.

my journal

my journal

my journal

my journal

my journal

my journal

my journal

my journal

my journal

my journal

my journal

my journal

my journal

my journal

my journal

my journal

my journal

my journal

my journal

my journal

my journal

my journal

my journal

my journal

my journal

my journal

my journal

my journal

my journal

my journal

my journal

my journal

my journal

my journal

my journal

my journal

TIME TO SOAR

As this chapter of your transformative journey concludes within the pages of Elevate Your Essence: The Confidence Catalyst of Goal Setting, realize that you've taken an awe-inspiring leap towards a more empowered version of yourself.

Now, armed with your penned dreams, your clarified visions, and your structured goals, you possess a roadmap to ascend the peaks of self-confidence. This journal was your compass, guiding you to the core of your aspirations and unveiling the architect of your own confidence.

Remember, the story doesn't end here. It's a prologue to the epic saga of your achievements. Carry the vigor of your goals in your heart and let your steps echo with the unwavering belief in your potential. Let each goal achieved fuel the fire of your ambition.

Your essence has been elevated, but this is just the genesis. The horizon of your possibilities is vast, and the canvas of your destiny eagerly awaits your masterstrokes. You are now equipped to face the world with an unshakable resolve and a newfound belief in your capabilities.

Embrace the challenge, embrace the victories, and above all, embrace the magnificent, confident you. For your journey has just begun, and the world is yet to witness the astounding impact of your indomitable spirit.

Step forth boldly, for you are now the captain of your fate, the master of your destiny. May your sails catch the winds of ambition, propelling you towards unparalleled success. The future is yours to conquer. Onward, champion of your dreams!

Discover the essence of empowerment with MeEvolv Journals & Planners, specially crafted for women of color. Our collection resonates with the unique journeys, dreams, and aspirations of every vibrant woman out there. MeEvolv Journals & Planners are crafted with precision and passion, our collection is designed to guide you through every step of your evolution. Whether you're setting goals, tracking progress, or simply seeking clarity, MeEvolv is your companion in the quest for a better you. Dive deep into self-reflection, plan your days with purpose, and watch yourself evolve. Continue your journey with MeEvolv today. Visit www.MeEvolv.com for a full list of our products.